CW01163575

inspire to teach

A Kids Guide to Becoming a Teacher

sarah michaels

Copyright © 2023 by Sarah Michaels

All rights reserved.

No part of this book may be reproduced in any form or by any electronic or mechanical means, including information storage and retrieval systems, without written permission from the author, except for the use of brief quotations in a book review.

contents

Introduction	5
1. WHAT IS A TEACHER?	9
The Many Hats of a Teacher: Roles, Responsibilities, and Remarkable Influence	9
2. WHY PEOPLE CHOOSE TO TEACH	13
The Spark That Ignites a Teacher's Journey	13
3. THE DIFFERENT KINDS OF TEACHERS	17
Exploring the Diverse Roles of Educators	17
4. A DAY IN THE LIFE OF A TEACHER	21
Join a Teacher on Their Daily Journey	21
5. THE SKILLS AND TRAITS OF A SUCCESSFUL TEACHER	25
The Teacher's Toolkit	25
6. THE EDUCATION PATHWAY TO BECOMING A TEACHER	29
From Student to Teacher	29
7. CHOOSING A SUBJECT SPECIALITY	33
Finding Your Niche: Choosing the Grade and Subject to Teach	33
8. STUDENT TEACHING AND INTERNSHIPS	37
Stepping into the Classroom	37
9. FINDING YOUR FIRST TEACHING JOB	41
The Journey to Your First Classroom	41

10. THE CHALLENGES AND REWARDS OF TEACHING	45
The Ups and Downs of Teaching	45
11. CONTINUING EDUCATION AND PROFESSIONAL DEVELOPMENT	49
The Never-Ending Adventure	49
12. REAL-LIFE TEACHER STORIES	53
Through Their Eyes	53
Conclusion	57

introduction

let's start at the very beginning: welcome to the world of teaching

Hello, young explorers of the vast universe of professions! Get comfy, and let's embark on an exciting adventure together. This journey we're about to take? It's all about a truly magical profession – teaching.

Yes, you heard it right, teaching! You might be thinking, "But I go to school to learn, not to teach." Or, "Isn't teaching what adults do?" True, but let's switch up our thinking caps for a moment. Imagine a world where you're the one leading the class, sharing knowledge, and helping others uncover the mysteries of math, the wonders of writing, the marvels of music, the magic of history, or the secrets of science. Intriguing, isn't it?

Introduction

The journey to becoming a teacher is a thrilling one, filled with learning, discovery, challenges, and immense satisfaction. And guess what? We're going to explore that world together, right here in this book. Excited? Let's get started!

To begin with, let's think about what a teacher really is. Picture your favorite teacher for a moment. What is it about them that you like the most? Is it the way they explain complicated concepts? Or how they always have a kind word to share? Or maybe it's the way they turn an ordinary day into an exciting adventure filled with new knowledge? Well, all these and more make a teacher!

A teacher is a guide, a mentor, a friend, and often, a life-changer. They're the ones who explain how numbers and letters work, why the earth revolves around the sun, or how to express ourselves in words or art. But their job doesn't stop at simply sharing information. They inspire us, encourage us, help us when we stumble, and celebrate with us when we succeed. They shape our minds, our attitudes, and often, our futures. In a nutshell, teachers have one of the most impactful jobs in the world.

Let's think about it. How many times have you found yourself saying, "Ah-ha, now I get it!" after a teacher explained something you'd been struggling to understand? Those "Ah -ha!" moments are powerful,

Introduction

aren't they? They open up new worlds and possibilities, don't they? Teachers have the unique ability to create these moments every day.

Now, I know what you might be wondering: "Why teaching? There are so many other professions out there. What makes teaching special?" Great question! In fact, that's exactly what we're going to explore in this book.

Remember, teaching is not just a profession—it's a calling. Teachers don't just teach; they shape the future. Think about it—every engineer, artist, astronaut, or president sat in a classroom once, learning from a teacher. Each of these individuals needed a teacher to guide them on their path to success. In this way, teachers play a big part in building the world of tomorrow.

So why write a whole book about becoming a teacher? Because we believe that teaching is more than a job—it's a journey. And it's a journey that starts not in college, not in high school, but right now. Yes, you, at your age, can start on the path to becoming a fantastic teacher.

This book will be your map. It's going to help you understand what teaching is all about and what it takes to be a great teacher. But that's not all! It will also guide you through the steps you can take right now, at your age, to prepare for a future in teaching. It will provide

Introduction

you with ideas, activities, and tips to help you develop the skills and knowledge that great teachers possess.

We are going to peek into the everyday life of a teacher and explore what they do. We'll learn about the challenges they face and the rewards they earn. We're also going to hear real-life stories from teachers around the world, learning from their experiences and their wisdom. And guess what? By the end of this book, you'll have a clearer picture of whether teaching is the right profession for you!

And who knows? Maybe one day, you'll be the teacher, standing in front of a classroom full of curious minds, ready to guide them on their own learning journey. Imagine the thrill of seeing the sparkle of understanding in a student's eyes or the pride of seeing them overcome a challenge they thought was too big.

Isn't that exciting to think about? That's the magic of teaching. It's not just about the subjects you teach, but the lives you touch and the difference you make. And through this book, you'll find out if this is the adventure you'd like to embark upon. So, come along, future teachers, let's begin this enlightening expedition!

1 /
what is a teacher?

the many hats of a teacher: roles, responsibilities, and remarkable influence

BUCKLE up because we're going to journey into the core of our expedition: the thrilling world of being a teacher. You might think a teacher's job starts and ends in the classroom, right? Ah, but there's so much more to it! By the end of this chapter, you'll see how teachers are akin to superheroes, juggling a host of roles and responsibilities while making a significant impact on society. Ready to delve deeper? Let's dive in!

Firstly, let's clear up something important. Who is a teacher? You might answer, "Someone who teaches, duh!" Fair point. But let's look beyond the obvious. A teacher is a learner, a guide, a mentor, a friend, and sometimes, even a superhero! They wear many hats, and each one plays an essential role in helping students grow and learn.

One of the most critical roles of a teacher is, of course, an educator. They have the task of sharing knowledge and making tough topics easy to understand. They transform confusing equations into solvable puzzles and historical events into exciting stories. But teaching isn't just about sharing knowledge; it's about making learning exciting and creating a love for knowledge that lasts a lifetime.

Teachers are also coaches. Have you ever had trouble understanding a topic, and your teacher helped you through it? That's the coaching hat in action. They don't just explain things once and move on; they patiently guide students until they fully grasp the topic.

But that's not all! A teacher is also a mentor, someone who supports and inspires. They encourage you to dream big, work hard, and never give up. They celebrate your successes and help you learn from your failures. In other words, they don't just teach subjects; they teach life lessons.

Have you ever had a problem and turned to a teacher for advice? Then you've seen the 'friend' hat. Teachers can be excellent listeners, offering understanding, support, and sometimes, the right words you need to hear. They're there to cheer you on during your best days and lend a supportive shoulder on your tough ones.

Now, you might be wondering, with all these responsibilities, how do teachers impact society? Well, that's where the real magic happens.

Think about this: every leader, every inventor, every scientist, every artist, every person who has made a difference in the world was once a student. And who guided them along the way? You guessed it: teachers! Teachers have the incredible job of shaping the future by influencing young minds.

Every day, teachers help students learn more than just facts and figures. They teach essential values, like respect, empathy, and honesty. They encourage curiosity, creativity, and problem-solving. These are skills that students carry into their adult lives, influencing their careers, their relationships, and their role as citizens. That's a massive impact, wouldn't you agree?

Teachers play a vital part in creating a well-informed, responsible, and compassionate society. They instill a love for learning, encourage critical thinking, and promote the understanding of diverse cultures and viewpoints. By doing this, they help build communities that value knowledge, respect diversity, and strive for social good.

Doesn't that sound incredible? And to think, this all starts in a classroom, with a teacher. The power of teaching goes beyond the school, beyond the subjects, beyond the academic year. It spans into the future, influencing the leaders of tomorrow.

2 / why people choose to teach

the spark that ignites a teacher's journey

NOW THAT WE'VE explored what a teacher does and their impact on society, it's time to dive into the heart of the matter: Why do people become teachers? What is that spark that ignites the passion for this profession? This chapter is like a treasure hunt, where we'll uncover the golden motivations that inspire individuals to embark on the teaching journey. Ready to dig into this exciting exploration? Let's get started!

Firstly, let's think about it. Why would someone want to spend their days explaining math problems, correcting grammar mistakes, or teaching the difference between a cumulus and cirrus cloud? The answer lies in the magic that happens when a student's face lights up with understanding or when a challenging concept finally 'clicks'. It's about the joy that comes from witnessing a young mind grow and the satisfaction of knowing that you've played a part in that growth.

One of the main reasons people choose teaching is the love of learning. Teachers are learners at heart. They relish in the discovery of new ideas, the pursuit of knowledge, and the joy of sharing what they've learned with others. They're fascinated by the world and find immense pleasure in unveiling its wonders to young learners.

Another key motivation is the desire to make a difference. Teaching is one of the few professions where you can see the direct impact of your work. Teachers help shape the next generation, influencing students' lives in big and small ways. They guide students to discover their talents, build their confidence, and pursue their dreams. The knowledge that they are playing a part in shaping the future is a powerful motivator for many teachers.

Then there's the love for a particular subject. Some people are so passionate about math, science, literature, or art that they want to share that passion with others. They want to ignite the same enthusiasm in their students and show them how fascinating their subject can be. And there's nothing quite like the excitement of seeing a student develop a newfound appreciation for a subject they once found dull or difficult.

Moreover, teaching offers a chance for creativity. Every day brings new challenges and opportunities to think outside the box. Whether it's finding a unique way to explain a tough concept, creating an exciting project, or making lessons fun with games and activities, teachers often get to flex their creative muscles.

Finally, the sense of community in a school setting is a big draw for many teachers. Schools are vibrant places filled with energy, enthusiasm, and a shared commitment to learning. Teachers are part of a team, working together with other staff, parents, and students to create an environment where everyone can succeed.

As we uncover these motivations, it's clear that teaching isn't just about instructing or grading papers. It's about passion and purpose. It's about sparking curiosity, fostering a love of learning, and guiding young minds to reach their potential.

Remember, there's no one-size-fits-all answer to why people become teachers. Each individual has their unique blend of motivations. It could be one of the reasons we've discussed, a combination of a few, or something entirely different.

The important thing is that teaching comes from the

heart. It's a profession driven by a passion for learning, a desire to make a difference, and the joy of seeing students grow.

3 /
the different kinds of teachers

exploring the diverse roles of educators

AS WE CONTINUE our expedition into the world of teaching, we're going to uncover the different types of teachers out there. You might be thinking, "Aren't all teachers the same?" Well, not quite! Teachers come in different types, each with unique roles, skills, and specialities. Ready to explore these educational heroes? Let's set sail!

First on our list are elementary school teachers. They are like the conductors of a young learner's journey, often teaching a broad spectrum of subjects from reading and writing to math, science, and social studies. Think of them as the all-rounders, setting the foundation of a child's education. Their classrooms are filled with hands-on activities, colorful charts, and a sense of curiosity and wonder. The elementary teacher's role involves sparking a love of learning and building basic skills that students will use throughout their academic life.

Next, we have middle school teachers. They start to focus more on specific subjects. So, you'll have math teachers, English teachers, science teachers, and so on. Middle school is a time of big changes for students, so these teachers often play an essential role in guiding students through this challenging period. They dive deeper into their subjects, introducing more complex concepts and encouraging students to think critically.

Then there are high school teachers. They specialize even further in a particular subject like biology, algebra, literature, or history. High school teachers help students delve into advanced topics, preparing them for college and careers. They inspire in-depth discussions, independent thinking, and real-world connections.

Another unique type of teacher is the special education teacher. These superheroes work with students who have various special needs, from learning and physical disabilities to emotional and behavioral challenges. They adapt their teaching methods to suit each student's needs, making sure every learner gets the opportunity to reach their full potential. They're kind of like educational tailors, crafting learning experiences to fit each student perfectly.

Let's not forget about the vocational or career and technical education (CTE) teachers. They teach subjects related to a specific career or trade, such as culinary arts, auto repair, or digital media. Their classrooms might look like professional kitchens or auto shops, preparing students for specific careers after graduation.

And of course, there are many other types of teachers too! We have physical education teachers who keep students active and teach them about health and wellness. There are art and music teachers who inspire creativity and self-expression. There are language teachers, computer teachers, and even drama teachers!

The teaching world, as you can see, is as diverse as a rainbow. Each type of teacher has unique responsibilities, skills, and areas of expertise. But despite these differences, all teachers have a few things in common: a passion for learning, a dedication to their students, and the remarkable ability to inspire and educate.

Isn't it amazing to think about all the different types of teachers that make the world of education so vibrant and varied? And here's the exciting part: as you continue on this journey, you'll get to explore which type of teacher you might want to be. Would you enjoy setting a foundation for young learners as an elementary school teacher? Or perhaps guiding students through the challenges of adolescence as a middle school teacher? Maybe the world of special education or vocational training sparks your interest?

4 /
a day in the life of a teacher

join a teacher on their daily journey

ARE you ready for a time-traveling journey? In this chapter, we'll fast-forward into the future, accompanying a teacher through a typical day. Sounds exciting, right? So, grab your imaginary time-traveling helmet and let's explore the day-to-day adventures of being a teacher. Onward, time explorers!

Our journey begins bright and early in the morning. The sun is just peaking over the horizon as our teacher, let's call her Ms. Johnson, prepares for her day. She checks over her lesson plans one more time, making sure she's ready for each class. Her bag is filled with papers, books, and probably a few apple-shaped trinkets from students. With a quick gulp of coffee, she's off to school!

As she walks into the school, the hallways are quiet, but not for long. Ms. Johnson uses this peaceful time to organize her classroom. She sets up materials for the day's activities, checks the technology, and takes a moment to appreciate the calm before the storm of learning begins.

Once students start to trickle in, the room bursts into life. There are greetings, chatter, and the rustle of backpacks being unpacked. Ms. Johnson greets each student, answering questions, and ensuring everyone is ready to start the day.

The morning is filled with teaching. Ms. Johnson navigates through different subjects, from math equations to history discussions, science experiments, and creative writing. She uses various strategies to keep the lessons engaging. There are group activities, multimedia presentations, and even educational games. The classroom buzzes with activity as students participate in the learning journey.

In between lessons, Ms. Johnson is busy with a host of other tasks. She's checking in with students, answering questions, providing additional help, and managing the classroom. She's like a maestro conducting an orchestra, ensuring everything flows harmoniously.

Then comes lunchtime, a bustling break for

students but a busy period for our teacher. While students head to the cafeteria, Ms. Johnson might catch a quick bite while preparing for the afternoon lessons or meeting with other teachers to discuss student progress and plan future activities.

The afternoon continues with more teaching. There might be a special activity like a guest speaker, a field trip, or a class project. Throughout the day, Ms. Johnson adapts to the changing dynamics, keeping the learning environment lively and responsive to students' needs.

The final bell doesn't mean the end of Ms. Johnson's day. After waving goodbye to her students, she has papers to grade, lessons to plan, and emails to answer. She might also have meetings with parents or other teachers. Even after the students leave, there's still much work to be done.

As she finally heads home, the sun is setting, mirroring the morning's glow. Tired but satisfied, Ms. Johnson reflects on the day. There were challenges, certainly. Maybe a lesson didn't go as planned, or there was a tough question she couldn't answer. But there were also victories. The light bulb moments when a student understood a tough concept, or the smile from a student who finally felt confident in their abilities.

Every day in a teacher's life is a unique blend of

challenges and triumphs, of hard work and heartfelt moments. It's not always easy, but it's definitely rewarding.

5 /
the skills and traits of a successful teacher

the teacher's toolkit

NOW THAT WE'VE explored the day-to-day life of a teacher, it's time to dive into the special traits and skills that make a successful educator. These are the ingredients in a teacher's secret sauce, the tools in their toolkit, that allow them to inspire, guide, and shape young minds. Are you excited to discover what these are? Let's dive in!

First up in our toolkit is patience. Imagine you're explaining a tricky math problem to a student, and despite your best efforts, they just don't get it. A patient teacher won't get frustrated or give up. Instead, they will calmly try different approaches until that magical 'aha' moment arrives. Patience means understanding that everyone learns at their own pace and being ready to support students every step of the way.

Next, we have empathy. Empathy is like a superpower that lets teachers understand and share the feelings of their students. Did a student have a bad day? An empathetic teacher will notice, offering words of encouragement or adjusting their approach to help the student feel better. Empathy builds strong bonds between teachers and students, creating a supportive and caring learning environment.

Communication is another essential tool in our kit. As a teacher, you're like a translator, turning complex ideas into understandable concepts. A great teacher can explain things clearly and concisely, making even the most challenging topics approachable. But communication is not just about talking - it's also about listening. A teacher needs to listen to students' questions and concerns, opening a two-way street for learning and understanding.

Let's not forget organization. Teachers have a lot to juggle, from lesson plans to grading, meetings, and more. Being organized helps teachers manage their tasks efficiently, ensuring that everything runs smoothly. It also sets a positive example for students, teaching them the value of planning and structure.

Creativity is the spice in our teacher's toolkit. A

creative teacher can turn a dull topic into an exciting adventure. They might use storytelling, games, or hands-on activities to make learning fun and engaging. Creativity also helps teachers adapt to different learning styles, ensuring that every student can understand and succeed.

There are, of course, many more tools in a teacher's toolkit. Traits like flexibility, to adapt to unexpected situations; a love of learning, to stay updated and make learning exciting; and a sense of humor, to make the classroom a joyful place. Each teacher has their unique blend of skills and traits, their unique recipe for their secret sauce.

As you journey through this book, consider which of these skills and traits you already have. Perhaps you're a patient sibling who's always helping your younger brother with his homework. Maybe you're the empathetic friend who's always there to support your pals. Or the creative thinker who finds unique solutions to problems.

Remember, these skills and traits can be developed over time. Just like a master chef learning to cook, it takes practice and experience to become a master teacher. So don't worry if you're not a perfect communicator or organizer yet - you have plenty of time to learn and grow.

Being a teacher is about more than just knowing a subject; it's about having the right tools in your toolkit to inspire, guide, and support your students. As you continue exploring the world of teaching, keep these skills and traits in mind. They're the foundation upon which great teachers are built!

6 /
the education pathway to becoming a teacher

from student to teacher

BY NOW, we've explored what teaching is, the different types of teachers, what a teacher's day looks like, and the essential skills and traits teachers need. Now, let's delve into what it takes to officially become a teacher. We're going to climb the education ladder, exploring each step that leads to becoming a professional teacher. Are you ready for the ascent? Let's go!

Let's start with high school. If you're reading this, chances are you're already on this step or about to start. In high school, you should focus on doing well in all your classes, not just your favorites. Why, you ask? Because teachers often teach multiple subjects, especially in elementary school. So, having a broad knowledge base is a great start. Plus, doing well in school helps you get into a good college - the next step on our ladder.

So, let's move on to college! To become a teacher, you'll typically need to earn a bachelor's degree. This is a four-year degree that you get from a college or university. You might be thinking, "A bachelor's in what, exactly?" Well, future teachers often major in education. However, if you want to teach a specific subject, like English or Biology, you might major in that subject and take education classes as well.

Now, let's pause our climb for a moment. During your time in college, you'll also need to complete what's called 'student teaching.' This is a bit like being an apprentice wizard in the world of Hogwarts, except you're learning to wield a teacher's wand. You'll be placed in a real classroom, under the supervision of an experienced teacher. This gives you hands-on experience and a taste of what being a teacher is truly like.

. . .

Back to our ladder. After getting your bachelor's degree and completing your student teaching, the next step is getting certified or licensed. This is like getting a driver's license, but for teaching! Each state has its requirements for certification, but generally, it involves passing some exams to show you're ready to take the wheel in the classroom. And voila! You're now a certified teacher.

Now, some of you might be thinking, "Can we climb even higher?" Absolutely! Some teachers decide to earn a master's degree or even a doctorate in education. These advanced degrees can lead to higher salaries, leadership roles, or specialized positions, like a school counselor or administrator. It's like adding extra badges of honor to your teaching shield!

There you have it, future teachers! That's the typical educational journey to becoming a teacher. It might seem like a long climb, but remember, every step is an opportunity to learn, grow, and get closer to your dream of becoming a teacher.

. . .

And as you embark on this journey, remember that you're not alone. There are mentors, guides, and fellow climbers ready to support you. Whether you're puzzling over a math problem in high school, writing a research paper in college, or prepping for your certification exams, remember that every challenge is a stepping stone, leading you closer to your goal.

7 /
choosing a subject speciality

finding your niche: choosing the grade and subject to teach

WE'VE ALREADY COVERED some hefty topics about becoming a teacher, haven't we? By now, you know about the skills a teacher needs, the educational requirements, and even what a teacher's day looks like. But there's another important aspect to consider: What grade and subject do you want to teach? This chapter is all about helping you explore that crucial question. Are you ready? Let's dive in!

First, let's think about grades. Picture yourself as a teacher: Do you see tiny chairs and tables, colorful alphabets on the walls, and pint-sized students learning to read? Or do you see a laboratory filled with teenagers conducting experiments? The age of students you want to teach can greatly affect your teaching experience.

Elementary school teachers get to teach multiple subjects and play a crucial role in their students' early education. These young students are often eager and curious learners. It can be incredibly rewarding to watch them discover new concepts for the first time.

On the other hand, middle and high school teachers usually focus on one or two subjects. At this level, you can delve deeper into topics and have more complex discussions with your students. It can be exciting to watch your students' understanding evolve and to see them develop skills to explore subjects on their own.

Now, let's talk about subjects. Are you passionate about literature, always lost in a book? Or are you a math whiz, solving equations with ease? Maybe you're a history buff, fascinated by the events of the past. Or a science enthusiast, curious about how the world works. Your personal interests and strengths play a significant role in choosing what subject to teach.

But remember, teaching a subject isn't just about knowing it well. It's also about making it interesting and accessible for your students. Can you find fun ways to teach grammar rules? Can you explain algebra in a way that makes sense to everyone? Think about how you can make your favorite subject exciting for your students.

As you consider what grade and subject to teach, think about your strengths and preferences. Maybe you're great at explaining complex ideas, making you a good fit for older students. Perhaps you're patient and nurturing, ideal for working with younger kids. Or maybe you have a knack for making learning fun, perfect for any grade level!

Choosing the grade and subject to teach is like picking out your costume for a play. You need to find the role that fits you best, that lets you shine and make the most impact. And like a costume, your choice can change over time as you grow and learn more about yourself.

Finding the right fit may take some time, and that's okay! It's a journey of self-discovery. Use your experiences to guide you. Think back to your favorite teachers and what made their classes special. Consider your own time as a student and what you loved (or didn't love) about each grade.

And remember, the goal isn't to find the "perfect" grade or subject. There's no one-size-fits-all in teaching. The goal is to find the fit that's perfect for you, where you can use your unique skills and passion to make a difference.

So, future teachers, it's time for some soul-searching. As you climb the education ladder, take some time to reflect on these considerations. Think about where your passion lies, how you can best use your skills, and what kind of teacher you want to be.

8 /
student teaching and internships

stepping into the classroom

WE'VE BEEN on quite a journey together so far, haven't we? You've learned about what it means to be a teacher, the qualities and skills required, and even the educational path to becoming one. Now, let's discuss a vital part of your journey, a stage where you get to dip your toes into the world of teaching: student teaching and internships. Are you ready to step into the classroom? Let's go!

First, let's uncover the mystery behind the term 'student teaching.' It sounds a bit like you're a student and a teacher at the same time, doesn't it? And that's exactly what it is! Student teaching is a period during your college years when you'll step into a real classroom, work with actual students, and gain hands-on experience under the guidance of an experienced teacher.

Think of it like being a superhero sidekick. You get to learn from someone who's been saving the day (or in this case, teaching) for a while. They'll share their wisdom and give you a chance to try out your own teaching powers. And just like every sidekick has a chance to become a hero, every student teacher has the opportunity to become an inspiring educator.

Now, let's talk about internships. These are similar to student teaching but may include a broader range of experiences. For example, you might intern at an educational nonprofit, learning about education policy. Or you could work in an after-school program, gaining experience with different types of learners. Like student teaching, internships provide real-world experience and a chance to apply what you've learned in your classes.

. . .

So, why are student teaching and internships so important? Why not just learn everything from books and lectures? Well, imagine trying to learn how to ride a bike by reading about it. You can learn the theory, understand the mechanics, and even memorize all the safety rules. But until you actually climb onto a bike and start pedaling, you won't really know how to ride, will you? The same goes for teaching. Real-world experience helps you understand what teaching is truly like.

During your student teaching or internship, you'll face challenges that you can't find in textbooks. You'll learn to manage a classroom, create lesson plans, and adapt to unexpected situations. You'll discover how to connect with students, keep them engaged, and handle difficult behavior. And through it all, you'll grow as a teacher and as a person.

Plus, student teaching and internships can help you make important decisions about your future. You might find that you enjoy working with a certain age group or have a passion for a specific subject. Or you may discover a new interest, like special education or bilingual education. These experiences can guide you on your path to becoming the teacher you want to be.

Remember, every superhero has a beginning. They all start as sidekicks, learning the ropes and discovering their powers. And every successful teacher has a beginning, too. They all start as student teachers or interns, learning from experienced mentors and discovering their own teaching style.

9 / finding your first teaching job

the journey to your first classroom

BY NOW, you've learned about the adventure of becoming a teacher: the skills required, the education you'll need, and the hands-on experiences that will prepare you for the role. But once you've finished your education and training, how do you find your first teaching job? That's what this chapter is all about! Ready to dive in? Let's get started!

Let's start with job search strategies. Finding the right teaching job is a bit like going on a treasure hunt. You need to explore different paths, follow clues, and persevere until you find your treasure, the perfect job for you! So, where should you start looking?

There are plenty of resources available to you. Online job boards are a great place to start. Websites like SchoolSpring, EdWeek, and even general job sites like Indeed often list teaching positions. Don't forget about the websites of individual schools and school districts, too!

Networking is another important strategy. Reach out to the teachers and administrators you've met during your student teaching or internships. Attend education job fairs and join professional teaching organizations. Remember, you're not just looking for a job, you're joining a community of educators!

Now, let's talk about the application process. Once you find a job you're interested in, you'll need to submit an application. This usually includes a resume, where you list your education, experiences, and skills, and a cover letter, where you explain why you're interested in the job and how you'd be a great fit. Some applications may also require recommendation letters from people who can vouch for your skills and character.

It might feel a little daunting, but don't worry! Remember that this is your chance to show potential employers who you are. Make your application stand out by highlighting your unique experiences, sharing your teaching philosophy, and demonstrating your passion for education.

Once your application is submitted, you might be invited for an interview. This is your chance to shine!

You'll meet with a school administrator, and maybe a few teachers, to discuss your application and your fit for the role.

Interviews can be a little nerve-wracking, can't they? But think of it this way: It's your opportunity to share your excitement for teaching and to learn more about the school. You'll want to be prepared to answer questions about your teaching style, your experience with students, and how you handle classroom challenges.

But an interview isn't just about answering questions. It's also your chance to ask questions about the school, the students, and the job expectations. This will show your interest in the role and help you determine if the job is a good fit for you.

In this chapter, we've talked about how to find a teaching job, apply for it, and ace your interview. But remember, the goal isn't just to find any teaching job. It's to find the right job for you, where you can use your unique skills and passion to make a difference.

So, don't get discouraged if your job search takes a while. Like any treasure hunt, it requires patience, determination, and a bit of luck. But remember, at the end of your search, there's a classroom waiting for you, filled with eager students ready to learn from you.

10 /
the challenges and rewards of teaching

the ups and downs of teaching

WE'VE LEARNED SO MUCH TOGETHER about becoming a teacher, haven't we? We've discussed everything from what a teacher does, the qualities you'll need, the education path to take, to how you can find your first job. Now, it's time to talk about the journey you'll embark on once you're in the classroom. It's filled with many ups and downs, but don't worry, every challenge is accompanied by a reward that makes it all worth it. Ready to explore? Let's jump in!

Teaching, like any job, has its challenges. Some days, your lesson plans might not go as expected. You may struggle to manage classroom behavior, or find it tough to connect with a particular student. You might feel overwhelmed by the grading, the meetings, and the parent conferences. And let's not forget about the early mornings, late nights, and weekend work that often comes with the job.

These challenges might seem daunting, but don't fret. You know why? Because they're all part of the journey. They're the mountains you climb, and trust me, the view from the top is worth it. Each challenge you face is an opportunity to learn, to grow, and to become a better teacher. So when you encounter these bumps in the road, remember, they're not obstacles, they're stepping stones leading you towards becoming the teacher you aspire to be.

Navigating these challenges will take patience, resilience, and a bit of creativity. There's no one-size-fits-all solution, but there are strategies that can help. For example, if you're struggling with classroom management, seek advice from experienced teachers or turn to books and online resources. If you're feeling overwhelmed, practice time management techniques and don't hesitate to ask for help when needed.

Remember, every great teacher was once a beginner who faced similar challenges.

Now, let's shift gears and talk about the rewards, because teaching is full of them! There's the magic moment when a student's face lights up with understanding. The joy of watching a shy student find their voice. The pride of seeing your students work together to solve a difficult problem. There's the laughter, the curiosity, and the excitement that fills your classroom each day. And there's the satisfaction of knowing that you're making a difference in the lives of your students.

Teaching is about more than imparting knowledge; it's about inspiring a love of learning, fostering critical thinking, and nurturing future citizens. The rewards of teaching come in small, everyday moments and in the long-term success of your students. Seeing your students grow and flourish is a reward like no other.

Yes, teaching is a challenging profession, but the rewards make it worth it. In the classroom, every day is a new adventure. One day, you might be exploring the rainforest, the next, you're blasting off into space. One moment, you're a detective solving mysteries with your students, the next, you're an artist creating masterpieces. As a teacher, you have the power to ignite imaginations and open up a world of possibilities for your students.

So, my future teachers, as you embark on your journey into the world of education, remember this: every challenge is a stepping stone, every success a reward. The road might be bumpy at times, but the journey is a beautiful one. And at the end of each day, when you look at the eager faces of your students, you'll know that every challenge faced was worth it. Because you, dear future teachers, are making a difference, one student, one class, one school day at a time. And that, my friends, is the true reward of teaching.

11 / continuing education and professional development

the never-ending adventure

ARE you ready to embark on a new chapter of our learning adventure together? Today, we're going to talk about something super important in the world of teaching: lifelong learning and professional development. You might be wondering, "What exactly does that mean?" Don't worry, by the end of this chapter, you'll be experts! Let's dive right in!

Let's start with lifelong learning. Can you guess what it means? It's all in the name! Lifelong learning is about continuously learning new things throughout your life. Why is this important for teachers, you ask? Well, think about it this way. As teachers, our job is to help our students learn. But the world of knowledge is huge, and it's always expanding! New discoveries are made every day, new books are written, new technologies are invented... there's always something new to learn!

So, to be the best teachers we can be, we have to be lifelong learners ourselves. We have to stay curious, just like our students. We have to keep exploring, keep asking questions, and keep learning. That way, we can keep our lessons exciting, relevant, and up-to-date!

Now, let's talk about professional development. This is a bit like the "official" side of lifelong learning for teachers. Professional development includes all the formal ways that teachers continue to learn and grow in their careers. This might include attending workshops or conferences, taking additional courses or earning advanced degrees, participating in training programs, and even reading educational research.

Why is this essential for teachers? Well, remember how we talked about the challenges of teaching? Professional development can help us navigate those challenges. It can equip us with new strategies for teaching and classroom management, keep us informed about changes in education policy and practice, and even help us meet the specific needs of our students. Plus, it can open up opportunities for career advancement, like becoming a school counselor or principal!

You might be wondering, "But isn't being a teacher already a lot of work? How do teachers find the time for all this extra learning?" It's a great question! It can be a challenge, but many schools and districts offer support for professional development. They might host workshops, provide funding for courses, or even give teachers time off to pursue these opportunities. And remember, as lifelong learners, teachers find joy and excitement in these opportunities to learn and grow.

So, there you have it, my future teachers. Lifelong learning and professional development are like the secret ingredients to being an awesome teacher. They help us keep our knowledge fresh, our skills sharp, and our classrooms buzzing with excitement. They keep us ready to face challenges, and open doors to new opportunities. And best of all, they remind us of the joy of learning, the same joy we want to ignite in our students.

. . .

And just like that, we've added another chapter to our adventure of becoming a teacher. As you close this chapter, remember, in the world of teaching, the learning never ends. It's a continuous journey, filled with wonder, discovery, and growth. And that's what makes it such an exciting adventure!

12 /
real-life teacher stories

through their eyes

ARE you ready for a different kind of journey today? One that takes us into the lives of real teachers, their challenges, their victories, and the wisdom they've gathered along the way. We're about to dive into some truly inspiring stories. Let's get started!

Our first story comes from Ms. Harper, a middle school science teacher who always dreamed of going to space. While she never became an astronaut, she found a way to bring the cosmos right into her classroom. She once told me, "The greatest challenge was finding ways to make the vastness of space relatable to my students." She overcame this by creating a miniature solar system in her classroom and organized 'space missions' where her students would explore different planets. Her students became astronauts, right here on Earth! Her wisdom? "The universe is in our classrooms. As teachers, we just have to help our students see it."

Next, let's visit Mr. Sullivan, a high school math teacher. He shared, "I wasn't always good at math. In fact, I struggled with it in school." But that didn't stop him. Instead, it motivated him to help students who might be having a tough time, just like he did. He turned his challenge into a victory, becoming a beloved teacher who simplifies complex equations and makes learning math fun. His wisdom is simple yet powerful, "You don't have to be perfect at something to teach it. Sometimes, the best teachers are those who've struggled, for they understand their students better."

Our third story is about Ms. Nguyen, an elementary school teacher. She faced a big challenge when she started teaching a class with students from all different backgrounds. She felt unsure about how to connect with everyone. But instead of letting that challenge get her down, she turned her classroom into a celebration of diversity. They created a 'Culture Day,' where each student got a chance to share something special about their heritage. It was a big hit! Her wisdom? "Diversity isn't a challenge; it's a gift. Embrace it, and your classroom will become a rich tapestry of experiences."

Lastly, let's hear from Mr. Jackson, a special education teacher. He described his work as a constant balancing act, working to meet the varied needs of his students while ensuring they had the same opportunities as all other students. His biggest victory was seeing one of his students, who struggled with communication, deliver a speech at the end-of-year assembly. His wisdom for us? "Every student has potential. Our job as teachers is to provide the support they need to uncover it."

These stories are glimpses into the world of teaching, showing us that even though the journey has challenges, it's also filled with moments of victory, learning, and inspiration. Every teacher has a unique story, and one day, you will too.

conclusion

We've come a long way on this exciting adventure of becoming a teacher, haven't we? From understanding what a teacher does, exploring the different types of teachers, discussing the essential skills, walking through a teacher's day, to sharing inspiring stories, we've covered a lot of ground. And now, we've reached the final chapter of this book, but not the end of your journey.

This chapter is all about you, your dreams, and the incredible journey that lies ahead. So let's dive right in!

Firstly, let's talk about dreams. Every great journey begins with a dream, a goal that sparks a fire within us. Your dream might be to become a teacher, to inspire young minds, and make a positive impact in their lives. And if that's the case, then you're already on the right path!

Conclusion

Remember, dreams don't come true overnight. They require patience, effort, resilience, and an unwavering belief in oneself. And the path to your dream might not always be straight; there might be twists and turns, hills and valleys. There will be challenging moments, but those are the moments that make the journey worthwhile. Those are the moments that shape us into who we're meant to be.

Next, let's talk about the journey. Your journey to becoming a teacher won't be exactly like anyone else's. And that's the beauty of it. It's uniquely yours. Cherish each moment, each step, each victory, and each challenge. Every experience, every lesson, every story will contribute to the incredible teacher you will become.

And always remember, a teacher is not just a title or a job. It's a mission, a calling, a lifelong commitment to nurturing and empowering young minds. It's about sparking curiosity, instilling a love for learning, and shaping the future, one student at a time. And you, my future educators, are capable of making this meaningful impact.

Lastly, and most importantly, believe in yourself. Believe in your dreams, your abilities, and your potential to make a difference. You have what it takes to become a great teacher. You are brave, curious, and full of potential. And above all, you have a heart full of

Conclusion

passion for teaching, and that, my friends, is the most important ingredient of all.

So as we come to the end of this book, remember that this is not the end of your journey, but the beginning of an exciting adventure. You have the map, you have the compass, and you have your dreams to guide you.

Thank you for sharing this journey with me. I hope you carry these lessons, stories, and inspirations with you as you step into the world of teaching. Your adventure awaits, and I cannot wait to see the amazing teacher you will become.

So, until we meet again, keep learning, keep dreaming, and keep shining, my future teachers. You're about to embark on a journey that will change your life, and the lives of countless others. It's a wonderful journey, filled with discovery, growth, and endless possibilities. And I know you're ready for it.

Now, go forth, future educators, into your bright and exciting future. I can't wait to see all the amazing things you will do. The world needs teachers like you, teachers who care, who inspire, and who change lives. I believe in you. And I know you will make us proud.

Good luck, and remember, this is not goodbye, it's just see you later! Happy teaching!

Milton Keynes UK
Ingram Content Group UK Ltd.
UKHW021247191124
451300UK00008B/251